I Dream

Antonio 'GoodBrutha' Jones

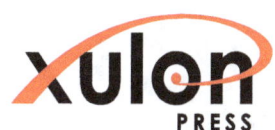
XULON PRESS

I Dream
A GoodBrutha Book
by Antonio 'GoodBrutha' Jones

Printed in the United States of America
Edited by Xulon Press.

ISBN 9781498468640

www.xulonpress.com

Author/Creator

GoodBrutha aka Antonio B Jones

Editor

Myeisha L Jones

Illustrator

GraphicsChef aka Morgan Evans

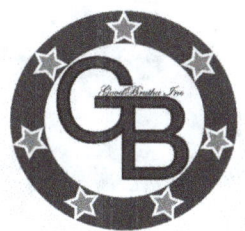

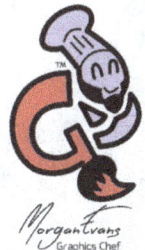

I dream that I am a fitness guru. All day long I work out.
I lift weights to work on the chest, back, shoulders, forearms and biceps.
My workouts consist of lots of running, lunges, squats, jumping jacks
and burpees to work out legs, thighs, calves and hips.
But most importantly, I have fun and eat healthy!

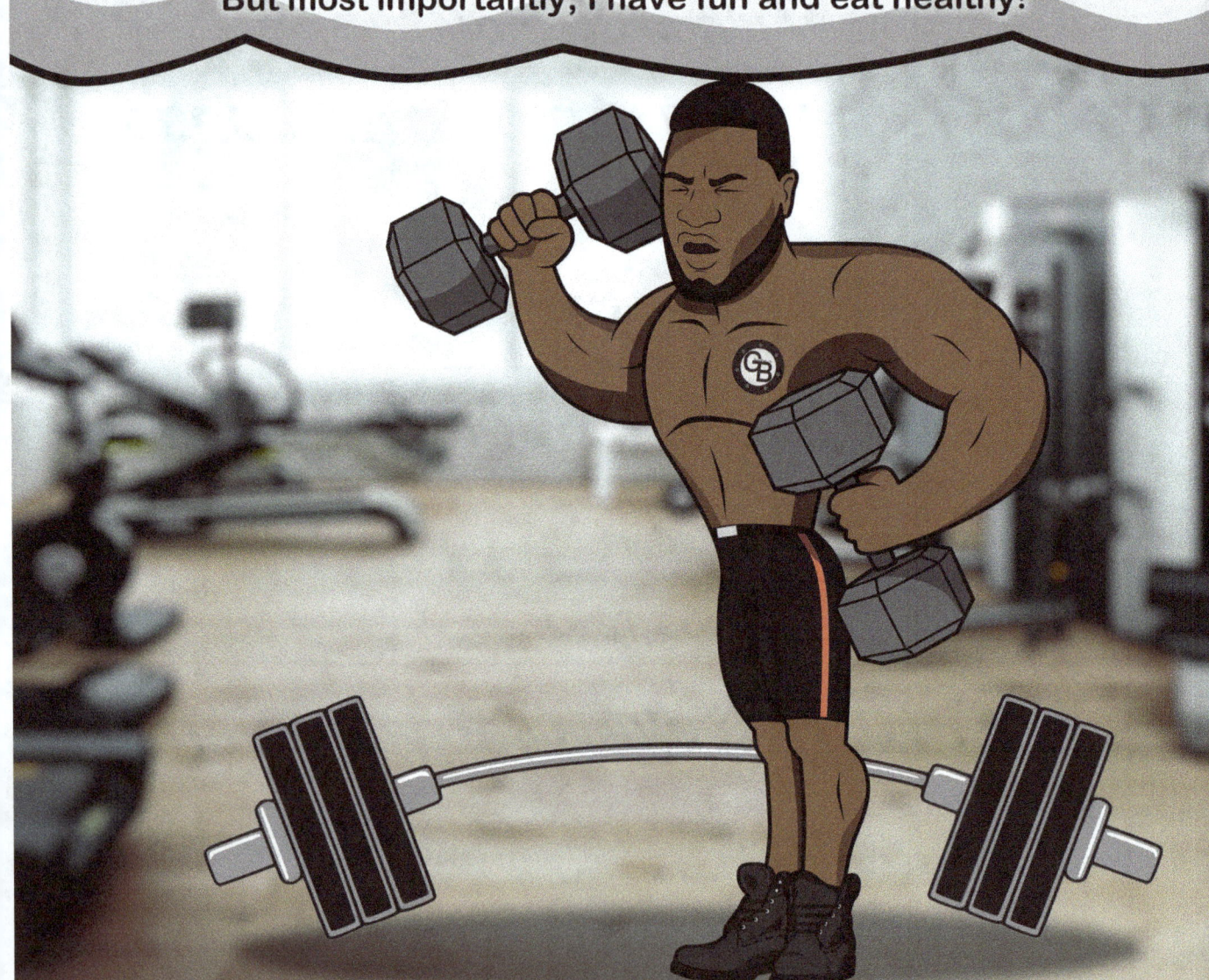

I dream I am great at riding dirt bikes. I travel the whole world and ride through all terrains, cities, states, and countries. I ask the locals to come out and ride with me. #BikeLife

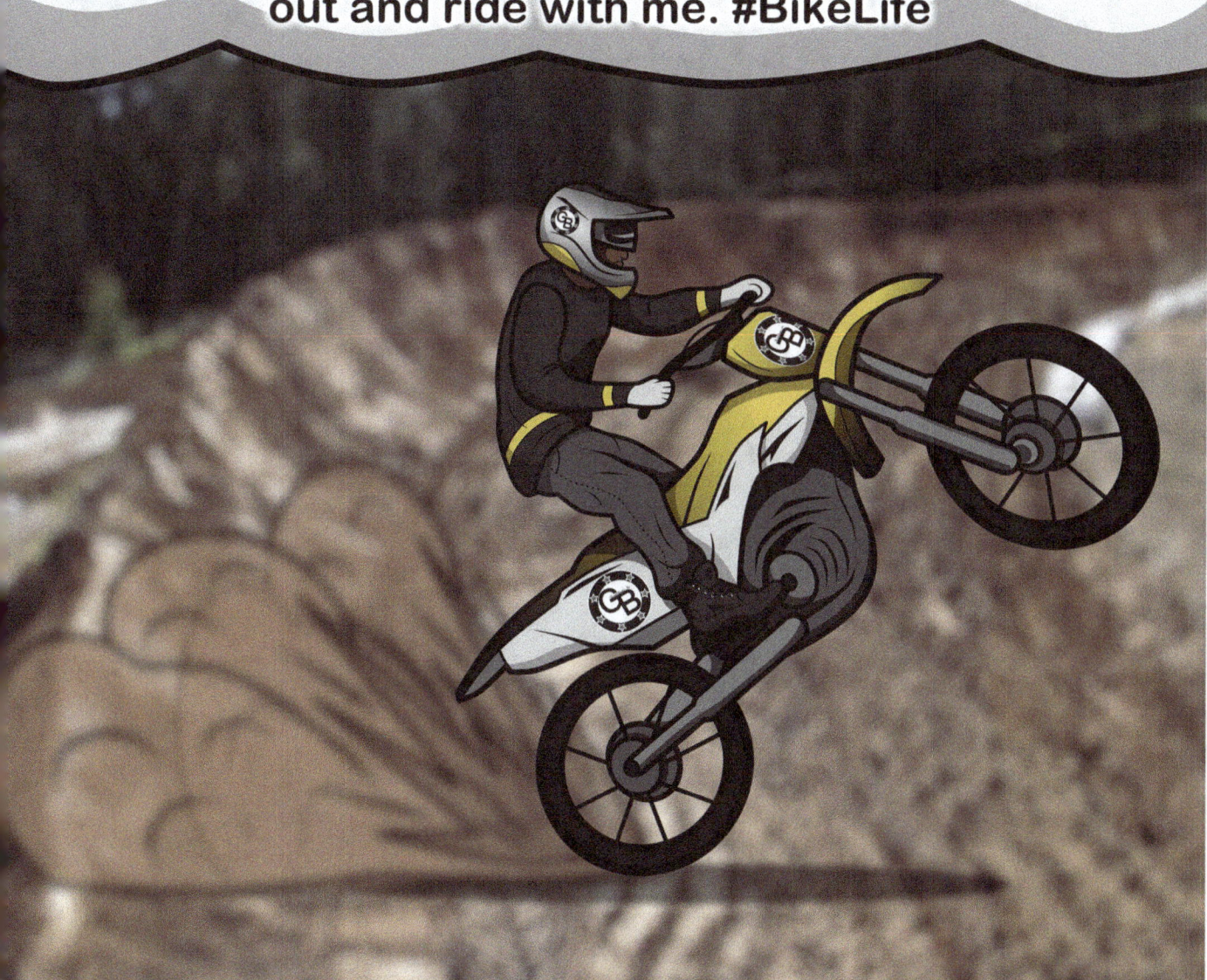

I dream that I am the smoothest transit operator in my region. People come from all over the world to ride the bus with me and see me navigate so gracefully through the city. I shall be called the "Smooth Operator".

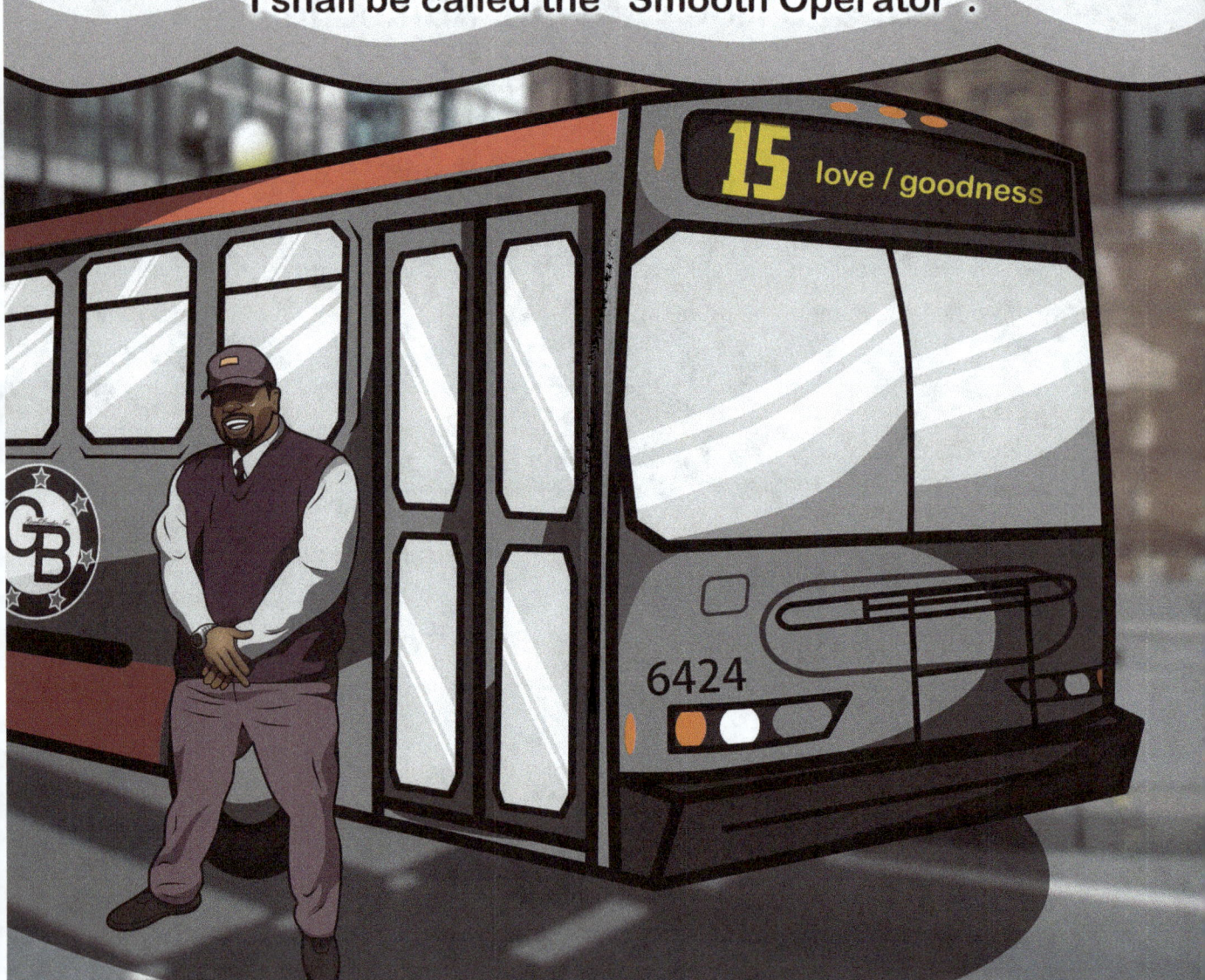

I dream that I am walking on the moon,
dancing with the stars and sliding down milky ways.
I am the bravest astronaut known to walk the Earth!

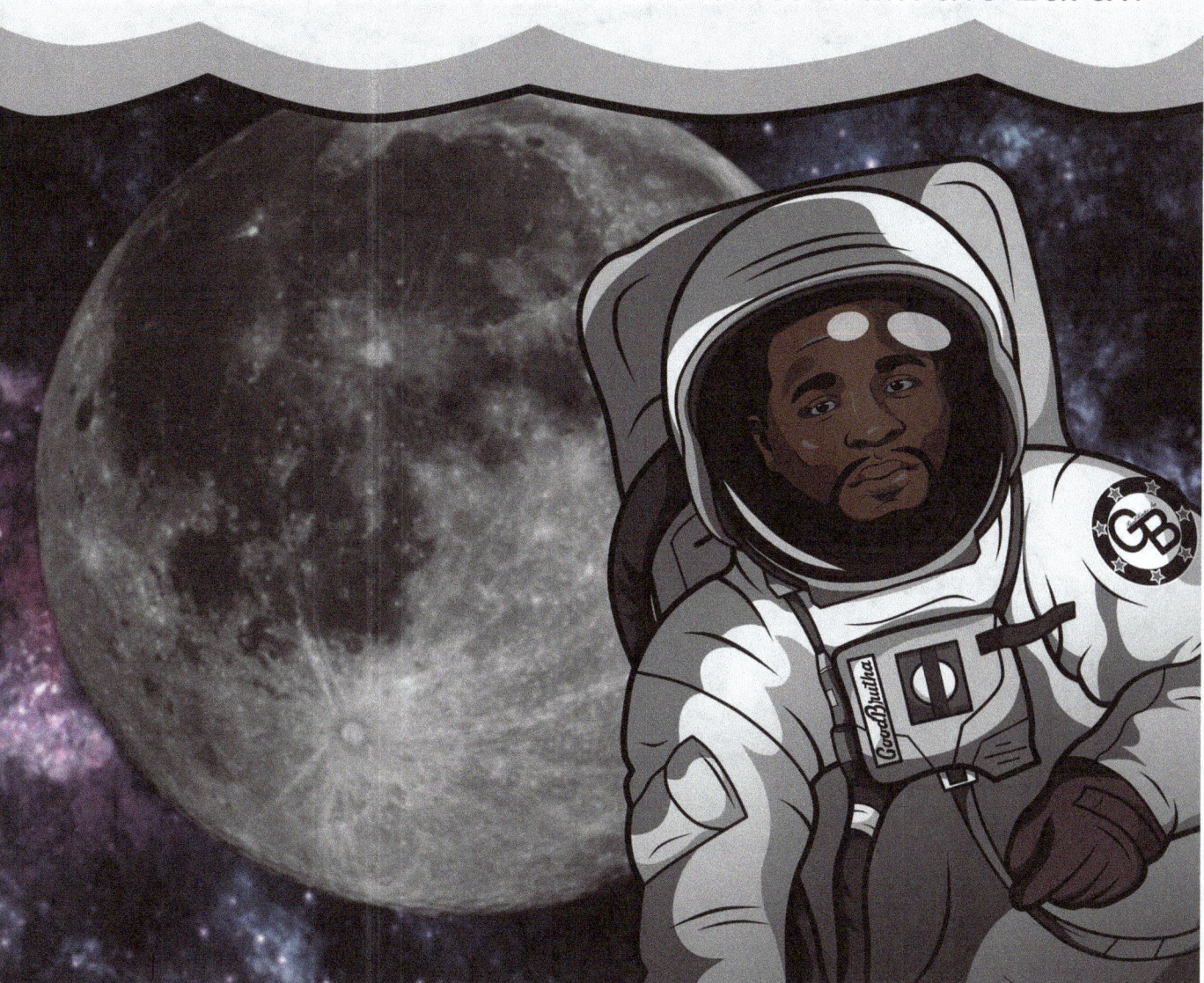

I dream that I am a scientist researching,
to find the right antidote to cure any sickness or disease.

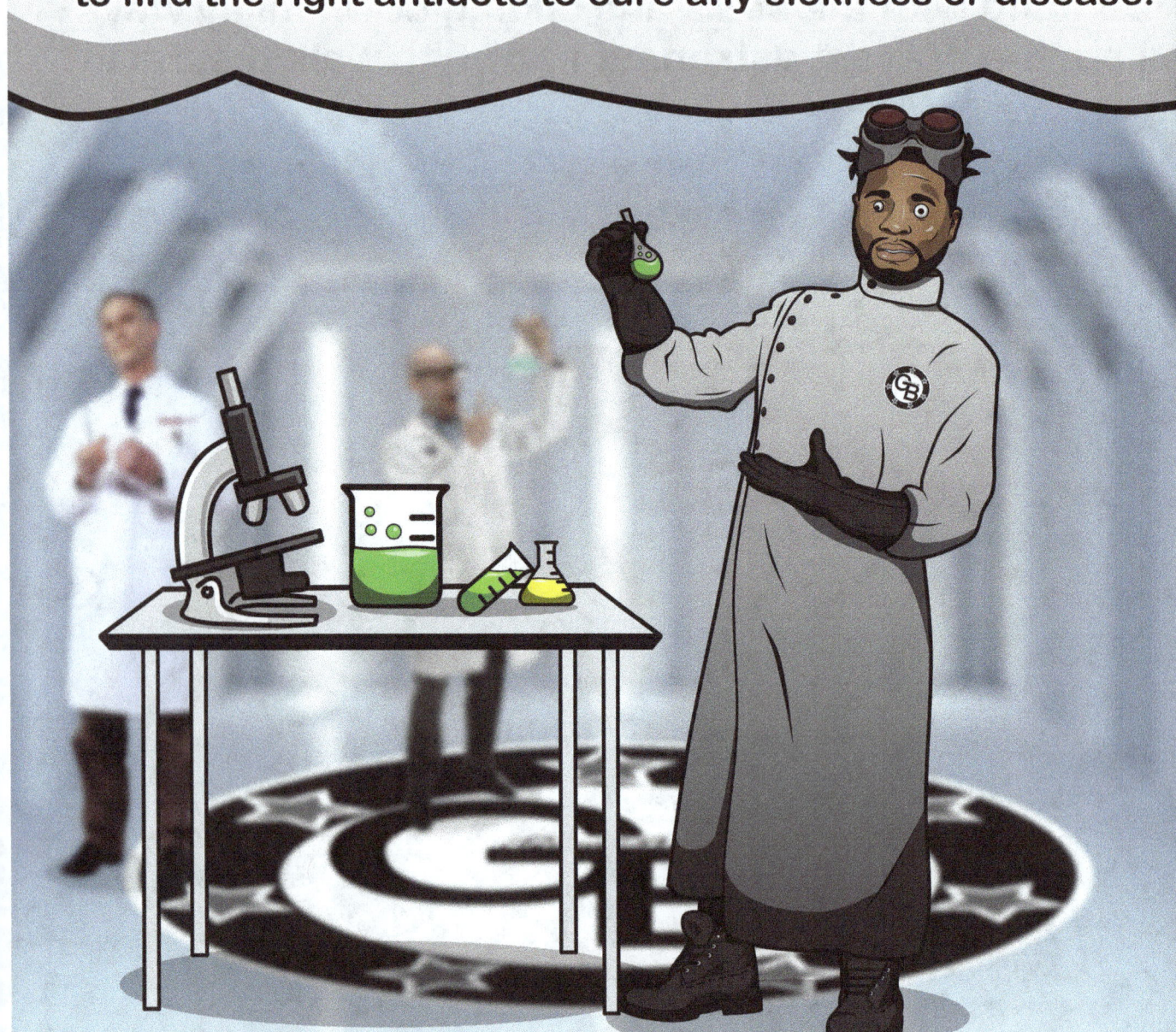

I dream that I am the biggest NBA star,
dunking in front of millions and millions of fans.

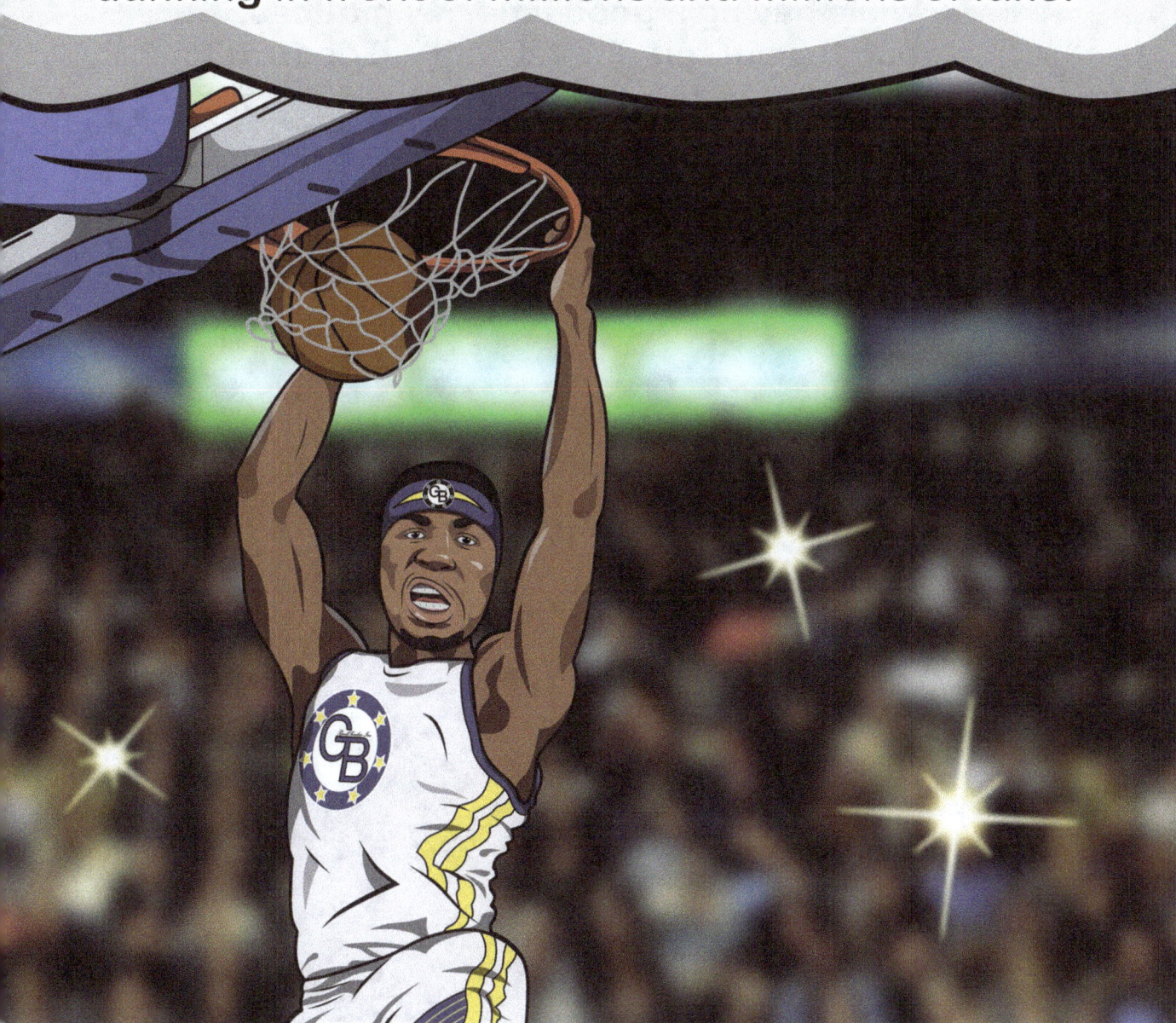

I dream that I own my own airlines - GoodBrutha Airlines: where you can eat good, feel good, and travel good, while having a good time. My motto is: "Be good to yourself. Travel with a GoodBrutha."

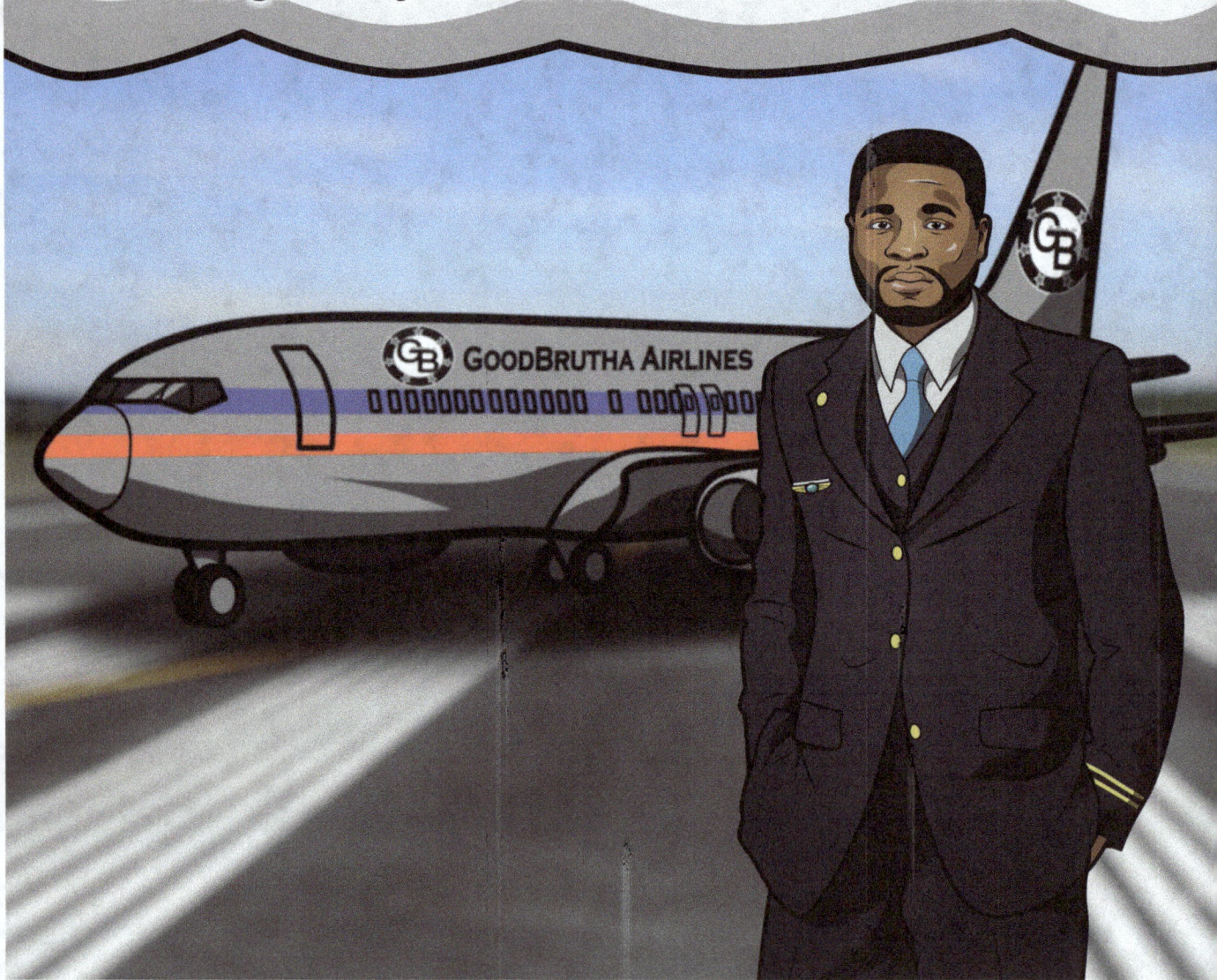

I dream that I am quick in agility, light on my feet, heavy with my hands, never missing a beat, skilled with my craft, passionate with my training, diligent in my work, blood, sweat, and dedication.

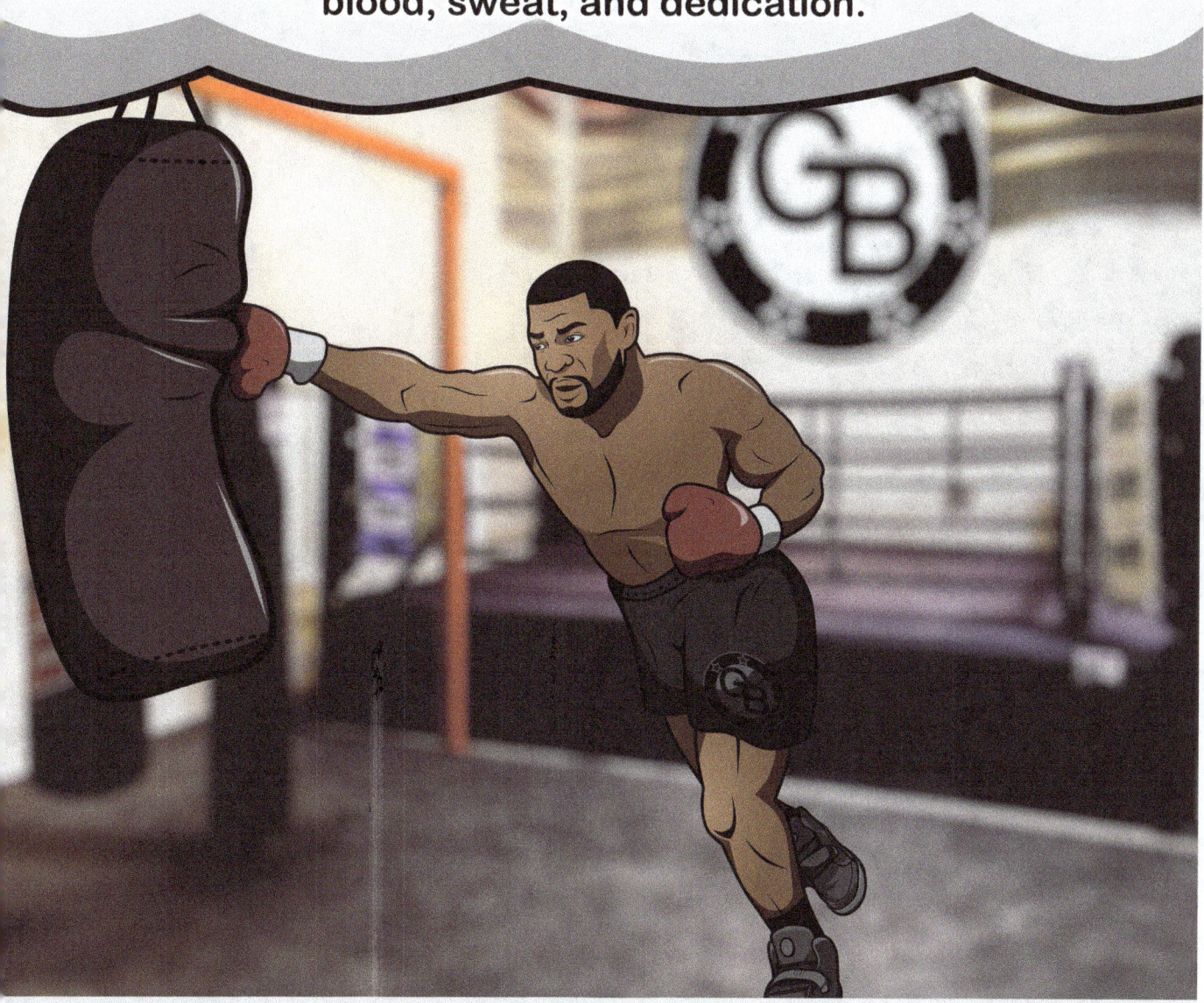

I dream I am a teacher who makes learning fun and exciting. We dig into history at its core and explore science at its purest form. We will explore math and find solutions to every equation

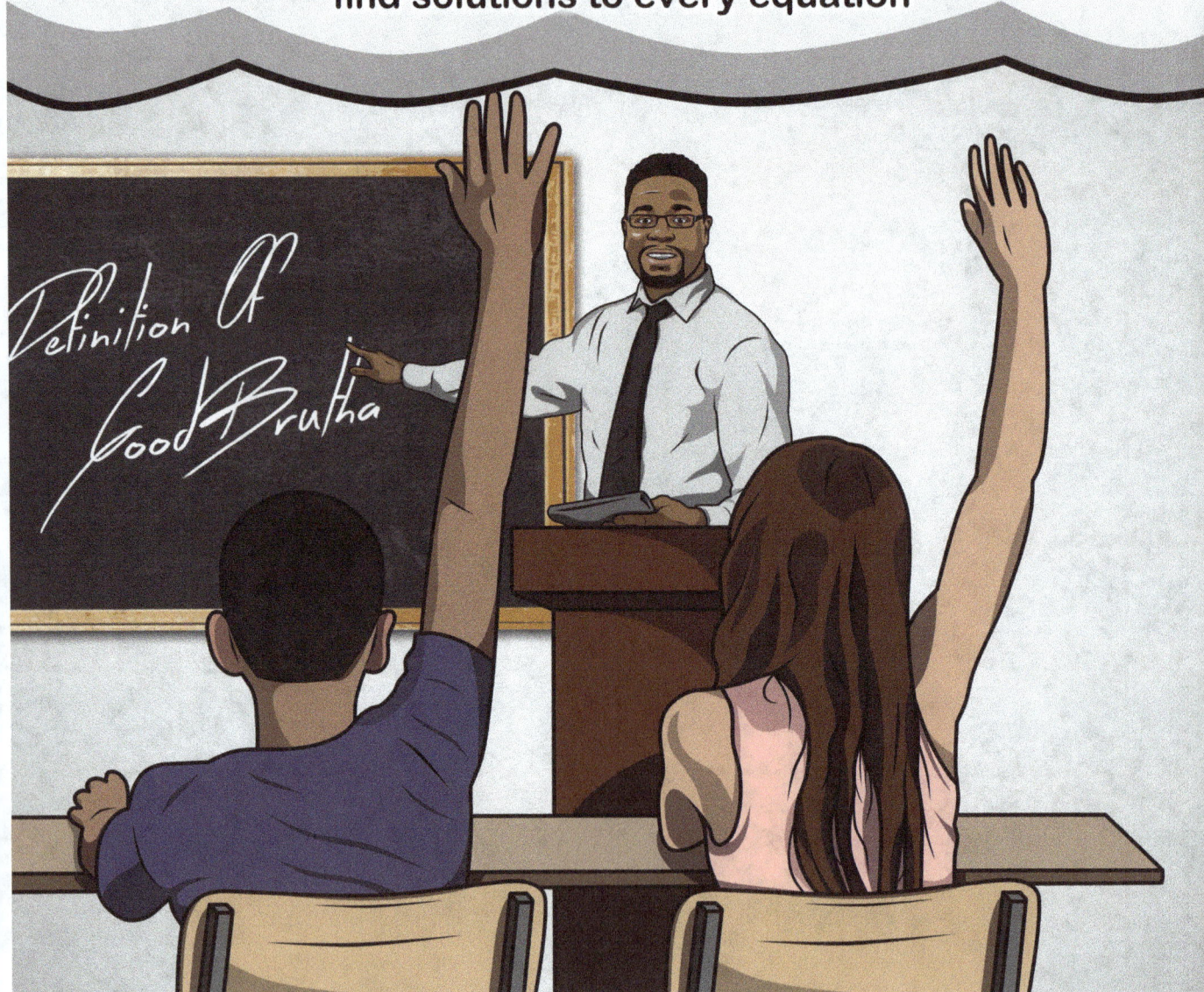

I dream that I am breaking down doors, running through burning buildings, searching for people that need to be rescued, carrying them to safety, and putting out fires. Oh yeah, I drive a big red truck!

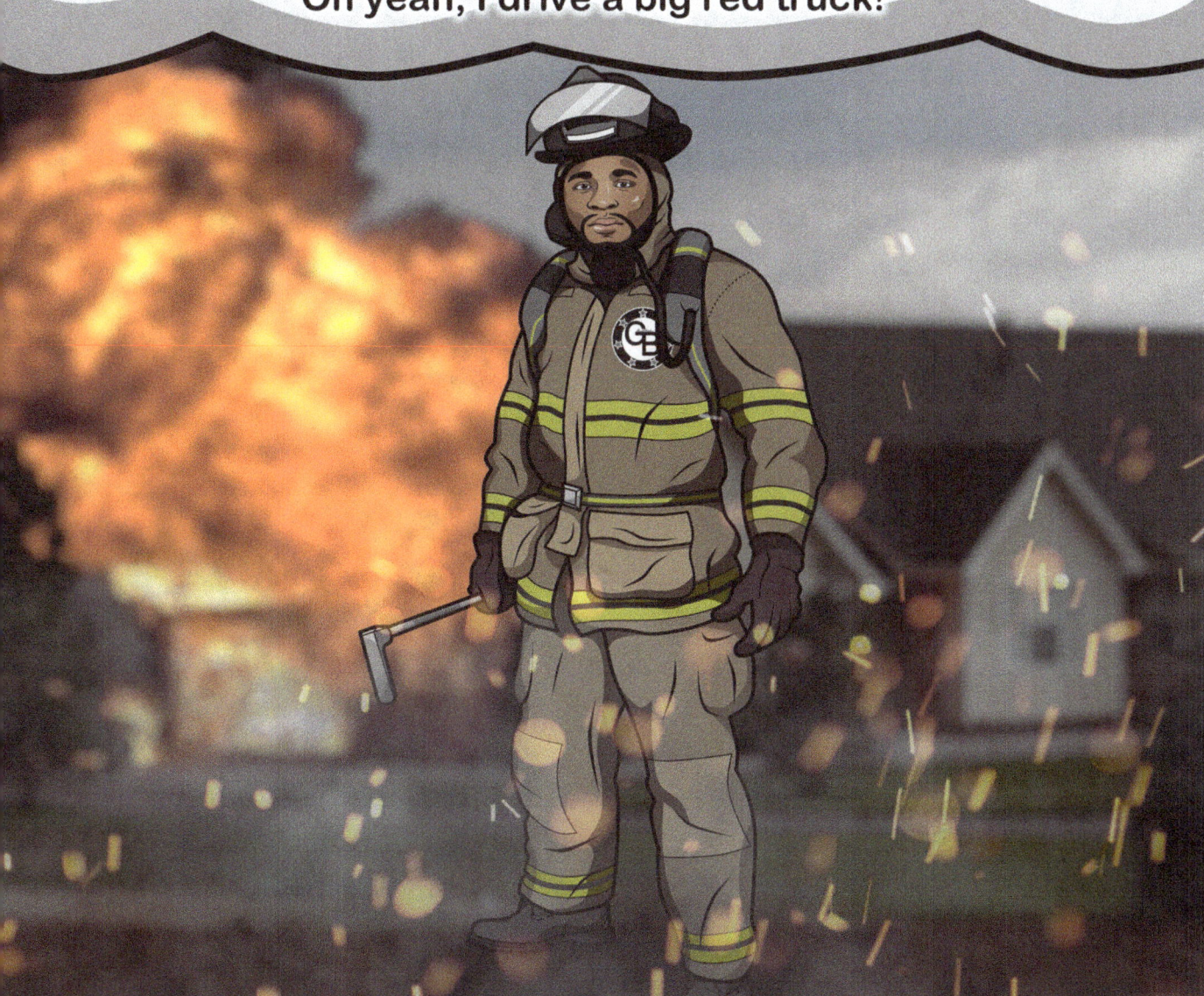

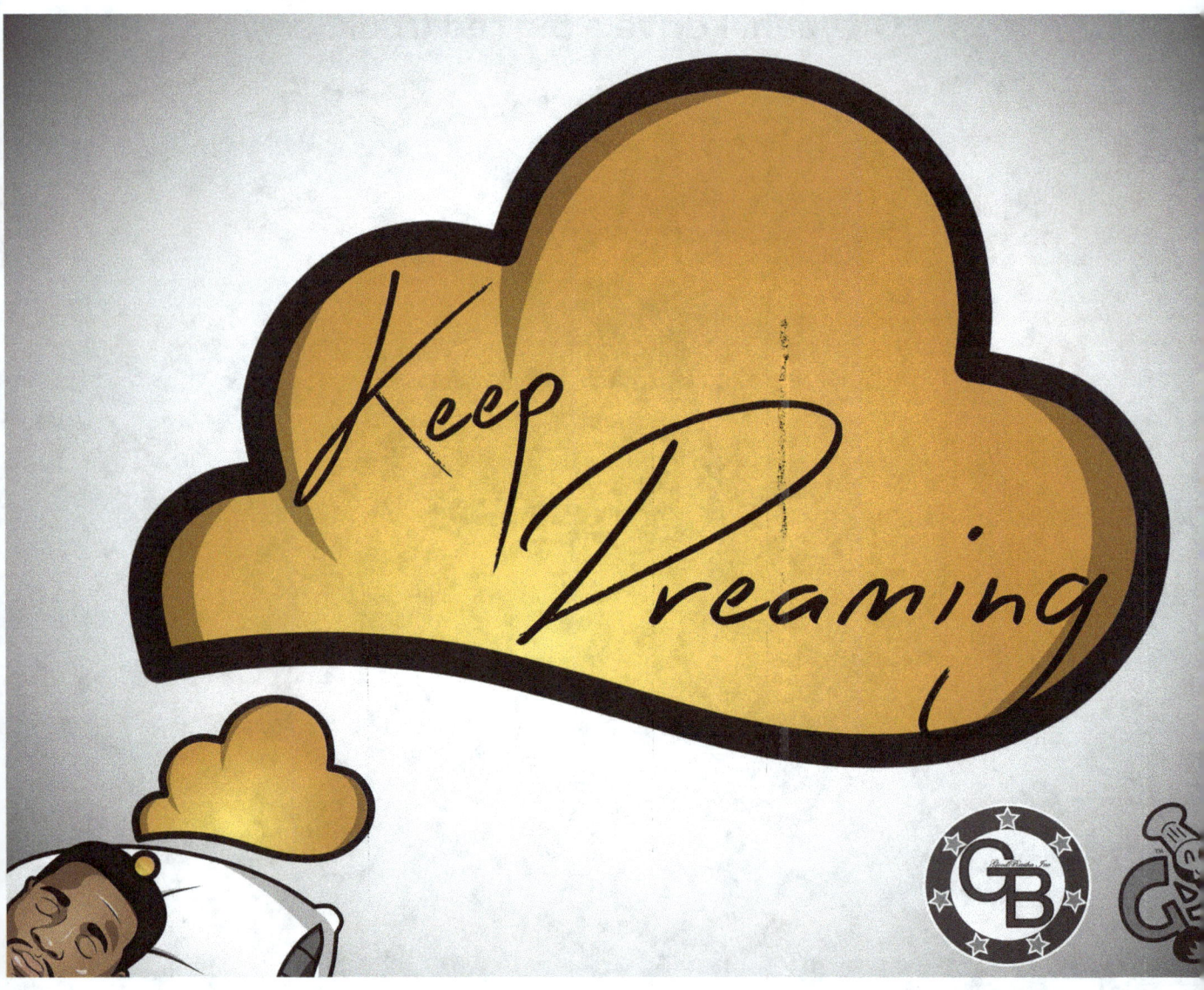

www.ingramcontent.com/pod-product-compliance
Lightning Source LLC
Chambersburg PA
CBHW081826170526
45167CB00008B/3559